GALE FOSTER

WIN THE DAY

**The Ultimate Guide on Winning Morning Habits
to Start the Day Right, Learn How You Can Perfectly Set Up
Your Entire Day to be Productive and Meaningful**

Descrierea CIP a Bibliotecii Naţionale a României
GALE FOSTER
   WIN THE DAY. The Ultimate Guide on Winning Morning Habits to Start the Day Right, Learn How You Can Perfectly Set Up Your Entire Day to be Productive and Meaningful / Gale Foster – Bucharest: Editura My Ebook, 2021
   ISBN

GALE FOSTER

WIN THE DAY

**The Ultimate Guide on Winning Morning Habits
to Start the Day Right, Learn How You Can Perfectly
Set Up Your Entire Day to be Productive and Meaningful**

My Ebook Publishing House
Bucharest, 2021

CONTENTS

INTRODUCTION

Have you been thinking about improving your productivity at work? Do you have an important project that you would like to give it your best shot? Are you wondering about how you can achieve your life goals and make that dream come true? Do you have a morning routine?

Having powerful morning habits that are engraved in your system and have become part of who you are is not only exciting but something worth pursuing. All you need is for you to audit yourself and take note of the habits that work for you. What areas of your life could use more stability?

Yes, it is not going to be easy! Some days will be easy, and others will be hard for you to set yourself up right. You may be ill or lose a loved one or you maybe you are just not in 'the mood.' Some of these things may break you and weigh you down. But does it have to be this way? Rather than allowing the ups and downs of life distract you from achieving your God-given purpose, why not take it as an opportunity for you to learn, pivot and give it a new perspective.

Having morning habits that you can stick to is the first step to developing grit and self-respect. In this book, you will learn the benefits of 7 golden morning habits that will help you win the day.

While you have your breakfast, think about the things that you would like to accomplish in the day. With a morning ritual, you have the magic to ease you into the day. You will be happier, more productive and have the confidence you need to address tough challenges that come your way. What will set you up for this? A winning morning ritual is what you need.

Chapter 1

Did you know that having a good morning routine sets the tone for the entire day? The truth is, there are more bad days than the good ones. There are days when we dialed into every little detail, and on most days, we simply react to other people's demands, feeling messed up and not in control!

In spite of the fact that having a good morning routine can be magical, the truth is that there is more to it than meets the eye! It is the science that you can incorporate into your life to reap extraordinary levels of productivity. The question however is "is there one right way to have to win the day?" Well, if you can achieve one good thing in the morning, it is as good as you have won the day and there is a high chance that you will enjoy the rest of the day.

Ask any productive person, and they will tell you that they have a morning routine that defines what they achieve during the day and hence, accounts for their success and productivity in whatever they do.

One thing that you have to understand is that morning are the most predictable parts of the day. But it only takes discipline and having a routine to reap the productivity that comes with it. All you have to do is tweak a few things here and there by adding on habits you would want to work on gradually to make a routine.

For instance, if you want to start working out, simply add it into your routine. When you feel down, you can write a few sentences about your thoughts and emotions. The whole point is to make that part of your lifestyle and have full control of your life. This is because, when you start your day with some routine and develop it into a habit, you will realize that you will gradually be adding positive thinking into your life. What better way to build your life than having positivity?

So, what are you waiting for? Come with me and let's learn the seven golden habits that will help you win your day.

Chapter 2

What are the benefits of having a morning routine?

According to several health experts, influencers and business owners around the globe, being successful is an indicator that you have a structured start to your day. If you review all the interviews on the Tim Ferris show, you will realize that almost 90% of the highly impactful members of the society have a morning routine. In other words, they have habits that they have cultivated over time and made it part of their lifestyle.

You may be thinking 'so what if you have a morning routine or habits?' Well, there are so many benefits that you stand to enjoy when you have morning habits, and the good news is that if you do not have one, you can easily build one for your mornings.

Core Benefits Include:

1. Self-discipline

Self-discipline is perhaps one of the most important benefits you get by just having a morning routine and habits. In fact, according to so many philosophers, there is evidence that shows that having that discipline of getting up every morning at the same time is a good foundation to kickstarting a good day. It carries over into the rest of the days in the week, and then months and years.

When you enforce an act of discipline at the start of the day, you will simply draw that discipline into various parts of your life. These include your mental focus, health, work, family and diet among others.

2. Time

The discipline of a morning habit and getting up early every day is one of the most practical aspects of extra time. In today's culture, time is considered the most valuable asset. If you don't believe me, look at the success that new time-saving technology like Uber, Amazon Prime, and Alexa's voice has.

The truth is, having that extra hour to your routine in the morning can be channeled into doing something productive. You can use that extra time to do something important to you that you normally overlook.

Limits Procrastination

I don't know about you, but to me, there is nothing worse than being rushed in the morning. But I bet this is pretty familiar to you too, right? Ever wondered why you feel rushed? Probably because you pressed the snooze button over and over until you are late?

Maybe, you spent too much time trying to make breakfast or put together your takeaway lunch? What you wake up to is realizing that you did not allocate adequate time for these activities, possibly because you allowed something else eats into their time.

Not having a morning routine simply throws you off the internal clock. This often happens when you do not have a definitive waking time. This is because you are constantly snoozing when the clock goes off. When you choose to hit the snooze button, you are procrastinating tasks even before you get out of bed.

This also applies when you procrastinate your urgent tasks to the next. You have to realize how toxic this can be to you. It does not only induce stress but most importantly, it serves as a barrier to attaining your goals and reaching your productivity limit. Therefore, it is important that you start creating reliable habits that are centered around your wake time so that you set the tone for your day, hence eliminate procrastination.

3. Helps lower anxiety

Over the last couple of months, I have been trying hard to expand my productivity limits so that it caters well to my evolving workload. To my surprise, waking up early boosts my productivity tenfold throughout the day. In fact, on the days when I get up as planned, I have ample time to ease into the day without necessarily rushing.

Stress is directly associated with increased levels of cortisol. This may lead to weight gain, anxiety, and several other health risks. If you have always been in a rush in the morning, try doing things differently tomorrow. Simply get up earlier than usual and take your time to get ready. Then stroll out the door and get to work. This goes a long way in lowering the chances of being anxious and developing stress in the morning.

It's much easier to dive into our to-do list without pressure. The act of checking off several tasks in the morning and creates the momentum that will help you push through the day. Trust me, it is the small wins that matter and pushes you to win big throughout the day.

We are constantly seeking for ways to maximize our potential and seizing new opportunities for growth each day. However, we must learn to adapt to changes that occur in everyday life so that we can eliminate the feeling of being overwhelmed, something that can strip us of continued productivity.

4. It gets rid of major decision-making

Regardless of how this sounds, the truth is that this is something very important. When you do not have a morning routine, you will not manage your time well, and this simply means that when there are important decisions to be made, you will spend most of the time agonizing over everything. This is something that can cause decision fatigue because of mental exhaustion.

You keep asking yourself conflicting questions that eventually flood your brain with unknowns. You do not need this in the morning, as it can be a huge detriment to the rest of the day. It attracts feelings of being overwhelmed and hence inhibiting your productivity.

When you establish stable morning habits that you do not have to think twice about, your morning becomes much simpler creating room for your brain to make informed decisions that will get you winning the entire day.

5. Mental toughness

Unfortunately, the society we live in today is too soft and fragile. This is because people try to find the easiest way out of every situation, most of which cause us to crumble. What you need for growth and development is a challenging setting.

Yes, taking that easy way out can be rewarding in the short- term, but have you stopped to ask yourself what this means in the long-run? It is true that waking up early each day may not be fun, but when you force yourself through this discipline and mental toughness, you are adequately ready for any challenge that life throws at you. The truth is, you will be standing when everyone else is not!

Chapter 3

The 7-morning habits of winning the day

It is important for you to bear in mind that morning habits will set you up for wins throughout the day. In other words, having a ritual that you stick to you no matter what becomes engraved in your system. This produces small wins that will ensure that you are steered in the right direction for the rest of the day. They create the positive momentum.

When morning habits are a lifestyle to you, you enjoy a path that is free of friction and strain. You start your day knowing that you are already a winner. For you to transform your life, you must first be willing to accept that habits can be replaced and that you have the power and responsibility to make a change to yours today. Start by thoughtfully designing your day so that you lay a strong foundation for a productive day.

Here are some of the habits that you set you winning the day for a very long time.

Habit 1: Beat the snooze button

Getting up is something that you struggle with at first, but all it takes to stop hitting the snooze button is tuning your mind to winning every day. There is a strong temptation and desire to hit the snooze button so that you can catch a few more wings in the morning. However, the good news is you can break that habit.

Each time your alarm goes off, tell yourself you are a winner by getting up and a loser if you snooze. Trust me; no one wants to carry the feeling of being a loser throughout the day. It worked for me, and it can work for you as well. You can start experimenting with other tactics as well to discover what works best for you.

Even though there is no single bulletproof solution to overcoming snoozing, you can counter the temptation of hitting the snooze button by simply experimenting different techniques. You may have tried countless methods with no success. Rather than beating yourself over spilled milk, cross off all failed methods and move on to the next attempt. You will eventually find one that works for you and when you do, stick to it.

18

Habit 2: Get up early

As you try hard to overcome the temptation of a snooze, it is important that you have a purpose to get up early. Understand that morning are times when you are fresh, have the energy and are away from external distractions of the world. During this time, there are not a lot of things competing for your undivided attention.

When you wake up earlier, you are at an advantage. However, if your wake-up time is 7 am, trying to wake up 5am instead can be extremely challenging. If you want to get up earlier than usual, try and do this gradually. Understand that it is a process and your whole body has to be ready for it. You can try with 30 minutes earlier than normal, then progressively increase to an hour, an hour-and-half until you eventually hit your target. Just remember to be realistic in every step that you take and make it count.

Make your bed

The first thing that most people do when they get up is making the bed. This is something quite simple and quick. This is something that I consider a second win to my morning routine. It simply adds a burst of achievement and productivity to your morning.

Why is this step an important part of your waking up? Well, the truth is, when you organize the environment you are in, you are stimulating your mind to be organized too. It is a simple step that adds clarity and calm in you, ensuring that you can stay sharp throughout the day.

Habit 3: Sweat it and immerse a positive state of mind

Fitness is a big part of a successful person's life. Engaging in simple mourning cardio, push-ups, jog or sit-ups can help you kickstart your day in style. Irrespective of what your fitness goals may be, working out as part of a morning routine is an excellent way to turn on your metabolism and brain. You will feel motivated, happy and full of energy that will steer you towards conquering the rest of the day and all activities that come with it.

After turning on your mind through physical exercise, it is important that you allow your mind to immerse in a positive thought process. Sit on a floor mat with your feet crossed. Close your eyes and think about the things that will bring positivity to your day. Do you want to be grateful, excited, focused, and inspired? Try and answer these questions in your mind. What are the things that you are grateful for today? What inspires you? What excites you?

Allowing your mind to tap into positive thoughts allows you to rid yourself of sadness and anxiety. In other words, you are training your mind to look forward to the best that the day has to offer. You will realize that, gradually, you will begin transforming into an enthusiastic optimist. By focusing on your top priorities each day, you allow yourself to make the most of your efforts and expertise on reaping tangible results.

Disconnect from the world

It is very important that you disconnect from the world around you. The best way to achieve this is by allowing yourself to reconnect with nature. You can take a walk around your garden for around 30 minutes. This is indeed one way in which you can exercise mindfulness. During the walk, try to collect your thoughts together to focus on the best parts of the day that lays ahead of you. You can also do yoga or choose to sit silently in the room, whatever works for you. All you need to do is to create a routine around your time so that you can achieve a level of comfort that blends well into your lifestyle. Whatever you do, make sure that you are focusing on the present rather than the past.

Habit 4: Write down your to-do list and goals you want to achieve today

To begin the journey towards achieving your dreams, the first thing is for you to identify exciting goals that will push you forward. In fact, according to a study from University in California, people who write down their goals are more likely to achieve them than those who didn't.

When you write down your goals, you are in increasing the effectiveness of realizing them. Incorporating this as part of your morning routine is a sign that you are declaring your intentions for the day. It crystallizes your goals in your mind so that they are engraved deeper into your subconscious brain. It is a signal to your brain that achieving these goals is important to you.

As a result, your brain will work hard towards achieving every goal by making sure that you treat every single project you handle during the day with the level of seriousness that will give you a win. In other words, your brain will push you towards realizing your dreams.

Habit 5: Focus on each task at a time

If you are handling a project, there are short-term and long-term goals. Each goal has some tasks/activities that you need to perform to realize that goal. Once you have this figured out in the previous step, you have to start focusing closer attention to each task. Pick one task at a time and focus on it.

It could be a new project, a new business idea or something that you just have to work on. When you allow your mind to focus on one task at a time, you are simply brainstorming on ideas that might be brilliant in being productive and successful. It simply tells the mind that these tasks are a top priority and the result should be beneficial to scaling the business. If you are taking a leadership role, think of various ways in which you can lead your team to win every day.

Habit 6: Visualize yourself living your dream life

How do you envision your dream life will be like? Every morning, take a few minutes to see yourself living your dream. Allow your dreams to sink deep into your mind and engage it for a couple of minutes using all your senses. Have you been dreaming of a vacation in Paris? Watch yourself enjoying that vacation with your loved ones and doing all the things you have in your checklist.

How do you feel walking the streets of Paris, shopping around, eating French food and sipping that glass of wine in one of the most beautiful cities in the world? What sound can you hear around you when taking that cup of cappuccino or Mocha in a café of your dream?

Yes, it may be hard to achieve ambitious life goals. You will encounter plateaus and valleys during the journey that might cause you to want to settle for an ordinary lifestyle. But you can start tapping into your mind by seeing yourself living your ideal day and life. When you start seeing yourself living your dream, you will start feeling a new rush of strength and energy that will motivate and inspire you to keep going.

It is only then that you will begin to have full clarity of the meaning and purpose of your goals in life. You will get a new perspective on how you can forge ahead and overcome the dark hours in your journey as you pursue your dreams with a lot of zeal.

Habit 7: Work towards your dreams

As part of a morning habit, it is important that you make progress towards accomplishing your biggest dreams before dive into the daily chores. Set aside at least 5 minutes to meditate on your dreams. As your dreams begin to grow, you can increase the amount of time that you spend working on them.

Rather than giving up the first few hours of your morning to running errands, channel that to a project that excites you. It could be that you are working on a new book project. Spend a few hours writing something. Simply use that time when you are fresh to fuel your will power before other *busy-nesses* of the day runs the tank dry. Take advantage of the full willpower you have in the morning to bring out tangible results of that project that you value most.

Remember that, if you channel your energy on activities that do not matter most in your life, you will find yourself going down a path that does not help you achieve your set goals and dreams. Ask yourself whether that project will lead you to the bigger picture. If it is a small part of the bigger picture, then you are guaranteed that your efforts will yield fruit and that each step you take draws you closer to your destination.

When you eventually add the small wins together from the morning habits, you create a ripple of victories that will keep powering your days. It is these small wins that will give you more confidence and keep you equipped to handle every challenge that arises during the day. It really doesn't matter what how difficult these challenges are. Because if you have strong beliefs and great habits, you can achieve anything!

Chapter 4

Boost Your Self-Confidence

Another way to win the day is to build your self-confidence. At its most basic, confidence is knowing what you're good at. It's knowing the value you provide and conveying that value to others. But don't make the mistake of confusing this with arrogance which involves believing that you're better than others. On the other end of the spectrum, there is low self-esteem which involves believing you're less valuable than you think.

Building self-confidence is aiming for the middle way without going too far.

Whether it's personal life, career or social scenarios, confidence is something everyone needs in any given situation. It is how successful people overcome daily obstacles. But it doesn't happen by accident. If anything, it comes from repeated practice and small successes which then build into larger accomplishments.

The secret to building confidence is to include it in your life as a habit. It may be difficult because people are naturally inclined to fall back into old habits and feel insecure of taking on a new one. But it is by no means impossible. Even being short of confident is a habit in itself. So the only way to become more confident is to build it as a habit and then become comfortable with it.

This habit formation involves making changes, adopting new behaviors and takes time and energy. At the same time, the process also involves breaking away from old habits and developing new, productive ones.

Expert opinion holds that the best way of doing so is to start small. This makes any task seem easy to handle. So take a look at these seven hacks given here to get you started.

Chapter 5

Use Positive Affirmations

When life gets tough, it's great to seek advice from others around you. But perhaps the best person who can counsel you is you. For many people, the natural way to relieve anxiety is to engage in some self-talk. But it is the way you speak to yourself during this pep talk that makes real difference.

There is a two-pronged approach to this. First, think positive thoughts and pair them up with positive affirmations. Second, remove any negative thoughts holding you down.

Many of your emotions get determined by the way you talk to yourself throughout the day. If you don't deliberately and consciously talk to yourself in a positive manner, you'll start thinking about the things that make you unhappy, lower your confidence and cause you to worry. Most people have these automatic thinking patterns that are negative. Sometimes, these negatives become so deep-rooted that it can be hard to change them without awareness and effort.

There is little doubt that using positive affirmations harnesses positive thinking. Positive statements that you repeat to yourself can help you challenge and overcome self-sabotaging negative thoughts. If you feel skeptical about using positive affirmations just think about it another way. Just as regular exercise helps improve your physical health, positive affirmations can do the same for your mind and outlook.

Conclusion

You have to understand that your morning does not have to be rough. When you allow this to sink into your spirit, you will get up each morning with enthusiasm. You will position yourself to seize every opportunity that comes your way and putting your best to work for more productivity the entire day.

When you keep telling yourself that you can do something and do it well, it will keep you motivated and boost your confidence. Some research also shows that when you use positive affirmations while goal setting, they become more effective. Identify areas where you need affirmations such as feeling and looking more confident and make them compatible with your core values. Finding those that resonate with you will be the most effective.

The power of affirmations lies in repetition. Recite these daily when you need a boost or when you engage in negative thoughts. While these may not help you forget your shortcomings, or erase toxic influences from your life, they will help you dwell less on the negative and focus more on the positive.

The reason why it's important to remove negative thoughts is that too many of these can easily become self-fulfilling prophecies. When you talk yourself into believing that you're not good enough, these thoughts drag you down and keep you anchored there. Use affirmations to turn such negatives into positives. When negative self-talk makes you struggle, choose an affirmation that is the opposite of that thought or belief and put that into practice.

The most common way of practicing positive affirmations is in front of the mirror. While this may seem silly at first, you do establish a visual and psychological connection with yourself when doing so. By looking yourself in the eye and telling yourself you can do something, you create a stronger belief in that thought.

Experts will tell you that you need to feel the affirmation and not simply say it. This adds weights to your affirmation and makes it more effective.

Chapter 6

Meditate

The idea of meditation may seem counterintuitive right after mentioning exercise, for exercise pumps you up releasing endorphins whereas meditation aims to relax and calm the mind.

That said, meditation is a great tool to inspect your inner thoughts. After a good session, your faith in your abilities can reaffirm and help you get past any doubts. Research has established that the practice of meditation can help with stopping negative self-talk. It is this negative self-talk that is often behind a lack of self- confidence.

However, when you meditate, the practice trains your brain to disassociate yourself from the ongoing mental chatter inside your head. This mental chatter is also often the source holding you back from showing your full potential. Your mind is so caught up in debating with itself that it prevents you from taking actual action about things that bother you. But meditation makes you realize that you don't have to listen to the voice in your head at all times, and particularly when it focuses on the negative.

When you meditate, you can silence your inner critic to take the backseat and settle down. Instead swap that negative self-talk with positive thoughts to get your confidence back on track. While meditation doesn't mean controlling all your thoughts, it does involve reducing the control your thoughts have on you. For instance, when you start to doubt your abilities, your value as a person or even your appearance, your self-confidence will plummet. Put simply, these thoughts make you feel bad about yourself.

Yet when you try to shut these thoughts out or argue against them, you're giving them the attention they don't deserve and only making them seem more important than they really are. However, meditation teaches you to simply observe these thoughts and just accepting that they are there tends to weaken them. As such, you reduce the emotional hold these thoughts have on you which will also reduce the frequency of these recurring thoughts.

Continued meditation will also help you realize that these thoughts don't define you. Just because you think something doesn't make it true. Meditation teaches you to recognize these thoughts for what they are; just thoughts. They are not your reality or truth.

You can pair your meditation sessions with positive affirmations as mentioned earlier. Or try some visualization instead. Visualization makes for the perfect complement to meditation and can significantly improve results.

Studies show that the brain doesn't differentiate between a real memory and an imagined or visualized one. Instead, when you visualize something vividly and with emotion, you brain accepts it as it were real and the mind records it as a real memory. This is how visualization is used to overcome doubts and build confidence.

The practice is easy to incorporate intoa meditation session where you imagine a situation and your mind records it as a real memory. As such the situation becomes known and familiar to you, which means that you'll feel more confident going through it as you've already done so, although in just your mind.

Contrary to popular belief, meditation is not something that requires hours of sitting still quietly. So if you think that it would be impossible for you to meditate, then just keep in mind that certain types of meditation such as yoga also include movement. If you believe that people have to be either good or bad at meditating and you're the latter kind, then just remember that everyone needs practice to get better at meditation. While some people may have an easier time focusing than others, even wandering thoughts are a part of meditation. It doesn't mean that you are bad at it.

And finally, if the thought that meditation is all about controlling the mind is holding you back from trying out this practice, know that the opposite is actually true. Meditation is not about controlling all your thoughts but about realizing that all thoughts can't be fully controlled. Your mind is the way it is and you learn to accept it as is. This acceptance nullifies your negative thoughts and empowers you to let go of unwanted thoughts easier, including doubts about your confidence levels.

CONCLUSION

Yes, it may be daunting to overhaul the whole routine at once, but you don't have to. Start small and work your way up to becoming better each day - purpose to introduce new habits and practices gradually to make a more robust routine. Just remember, if you win the morning, you win the rest of your day. So, what is it going to be like for you this year? You are a champion, and all that matters is a win!

9 789533 081403

Printed by Libri Plureos GmbH in Hamburg, Germany